Arising
Sunflower.
Lost in Translation

Remy Antoinette

Book Cover: Kate Skelton
www.kateskelton.com

Interior design: Ines Monnet
www.inesbookformatter.com

Editor: Jessica Grace Coleman
www.colemanediting.co.uk

Illustrations copyright © Lakieshia Stapleton Jelenke, 2020

Paperback ISBN: 978-1649218315
Ebook ISBN: 978-164218292

Contents

Preface_____1

Processing_____3

Introversion_____7

Division_____13

False Imagery of the Outer Being_____17

Authorisation_____23

Review_____29

Repetition of Emotions_____31

Vocal Communication x Triangulation_____39

Wasps_____47

Almond Blossoms_____53

Lavender Essence for Amethyst_____59

Check-In_____63

Accountability_____65

Decorum_____71

Sunflower_____77

Metro Writing_____81

Mental Analysis_____85

Façade_____87

Biblical_____93

Acknowledgements_____101

About the Author_____103

Preface

Arising Sunflower. Lost in Translation is a collection of poetic quotes inspired by and created in an atmosphere of love, abundance, and commitment.

Several years ago, I began a spiritual and creative journey, which started with the suggestion: "Keep organising your life". I began journaling, a very fulfilling and satisfying activity which helps to keep my day-to-day life in order and fuels my creative process. The words set down on these pages were fashioned with the intention of sharing them with my readers; I hope you find something here that resonates with you. The inspiration for this book developed during a time of isolation in a foreign space. Experiences are what you make of them, both good and bad. You may be travelling a very lonely road in this life, but one thing I have learned is that it gets easier. Embrace life, in all its dysfunctional elements, and find joy in the world around you.

A large part of my isolation came from language and culture barriers, which made me feel mute. Amongst the sometimes tumultuous emotions of this time I found my poetry, beginning with my inner self and my observations of verbal and physical loneliness. Words – specifically poetry – became an outlet and a source of relief. Sadly, today's society is a form of structured chaos that leads to people becoming stagnant and feeling lost.

No one is immune; everyone has at one time in their lives experienced this, or is still a victim of it.

The book is divided into sections. Each title and subtitle reflect an underlying meaning and are open to interpretation, but my intention is to later analyse these quotes and micro-poems for my readers, from my own personal perception. Much of this material addresses the feeling of going insane, and overcoming this by finding an individualised safe space. Several exercises and action plans are included, enabling you to work on self and reflect.

These words may trigger different emotions within you. I hope that, by the end of the book, I will have evoked a feeling of reflection, perseverance, and rejoicing within you.

Processing

Diary Entry

From my remembrance,

Lack of confidence began with skin:

Irritation, agitation and stress.

Solar flares of broken skin.

Each prickle came with a question:

Will this ever disappear?

Glancing at old photographs,

That little girl is looking up at me,

Saying,

"You are amazing and have accomplished so much.

Do not be so hard on yourself!"

Self-reflection

Let these words resonate with you!

Reminisce!

How much of your childhood can you recall?

- **What can you see?**
- **What can you hear?**
- **What can you taste?**
- **What can you smell?**
- **And what can you feel?**

A trigger to an offset of feelings. The past does not define your future, but some bullets need to be ignited. The result can be explosive with an intensive recovery; this only builds strength.

Cont.
Current Diary Entry

A time suffering from really bad anxiety.

Life feels like it's at a standstill.

Everything is scattered, and nothing is secure.

Underestimating strength, being removed from your safety net.

Dwell on how this duration has flashed by.

Have faith and continue to push yourself to the next level.

Believe!

Opportunities will arise in your journey, for a purpose,

Somehow all at the right time.

22/07/2018

Introversion

Emotional Resilience

A stressful child continues to block out past experiences. Throughout
influential milestones, the most recent Aspects can be recalled.
Heart racing. Palms sweating.
Inhalation.
The pause between each breath gets closer and closer.
Never speaking.
Never highlighting sentiments.
Does this evolve into a state of oppression?
Resilience dimmed; inability to manage emotions
And toxicity emerges, in everyday situations.

Bubble Wrap

Walking bubble wrap,

Protecting a frail vase,

Which is fragile to fractures.

Can a broken vase be rectified?

Certainly, creating a beautiful mosaic,

An expressive piece of artwork

At its finest.

Failure vs. Self-Reliance

Create your goals and ambitions.

Organise and attend opportunities; they build your skills no matter what!

Never believe you've failed.

Failure is not possible.

Invest in a new pathway, if necessary.

Discuss availability with a positive role model.

Evaluate the positives and negatives.

Never say never.

Consider the final decision.

Evolve and continue to blossom.

Altruistic

altru:ˈɪstɪk/ adjective

Installing all life's problems in a box and fearing the results.

It's not possible for all this substance to be hoarded in a small surface area.

You have to be specific with what is 'entitled' and what is 'excess' luggage.

Creating your happiness is like a complex equation of:

(selfishness x communication) + courage – doubt – fear

along with many other adjectives and nouns = higher self.

Division

Millennials

As time passes, seconds roll into minutes,

Minutes into hours,

Hours into months

And months, into years.

Evaluate and observe.

Don't feel like you're the only one,

Feeling lost with life.

No sense of direction;

Working on developing your emotional stability

And refraining from the 'status quo'.

It may not be new knowledge.

A gentle reminder,

All systems create conformists.

Not everyone fits in these

Boxes and obtains a pro-active attitude

Towards structured learning.

Materialism is normal, to a certain extent,

Although it continues to benefit the elite.

Truth is, it leaves a sense of confusion.

How can millennials thrive in the workforce

When all they know is material success,

Qualifications, and 'being mollycoddled'?

Money motivated,
Bereft of affection.

The paper equivalent to trees.

Those who destroy a rainforest have no animosity.

Those who are tremendously affluent;

Could they trade places with those living

'On the breadline'?

Having no structure

And destroyed by famine.

Fairy Tale Endings

Planted with no stability, how does one search and know what to expect in another? Used, abused and broken; then rebuilding commenced, and the priority was to flourish. Through hail, thunder, and storm we sometimes have to comprehend the hardest path. You need to recognise your worth and not accept being treated as less, just for convenience.

Trust and believe that you were gracefully produced and deserve nothing but the best. There will be trials and tribulations within any journey, but you must communicate your needs, desires, and wants. It works both ways and your significant other should make you feel appreciated, loved, and content. If they don't live up to this, you have to change the momentum!

**False
Imagery
of the Outer Being**

Shadeism

Insults to the skin you're in,
Like anyone else can live your life.
Similar encounters can be negotiated,
But no experience is identical. Society is a
Construction site of false ego
And expectations.

Take pride in your value; reject prejudices.
Discreet to the discretion of subliminal messages.
All broken crayons can be utilised
And the distinction of shades nor tints
Are relevantly **irrelevant.**

Nurture

A typical seven days.

Unfolding for many eras.

Always for the preparation of a new manifestation.

Spontaneously here every three months, skipping cycles.

A deficiency in vitamins absorbed by the sun

And losing sight of basic needs, due to no resolution.

Although prescriptions become never-ending,

Medication only soothes the abnormality.

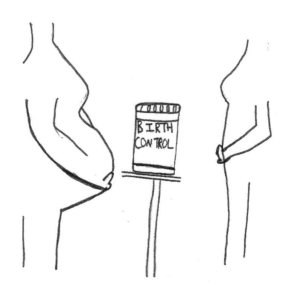

Salon

Breakage – from unconscious repression.

Salvage – from not completely starting again.

Compression – with moisture and maintenance.

Hydration and nutrients for – growth.

An aerial requires some sort of – protection.

Choose what is convenient for you.

Hummingbirds

Hummingbirds sustain the world's fastest metabolism.

Consuming their own body mass

With no rise in body weight.

The consumption of protein is important,

Yet they sustain a very limited diet.

'*Petiteness*' does not differentiate one's capability;

Naturally be a hummingbird at a flower.

Authorisation

Pharmacies

An overdose for society;

Concrete to every corner.

Unfortunately,

A dispensary for the needy.

And creating a captivity

To opioids.

15/09/18

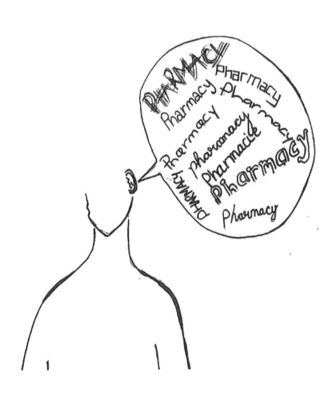

Grounding Your Foundation

Grass can grow through concrete.

Cracks enforce the relief of drainage,

So sunflowers can be planted.

Arising via the nourishment of topsoil.

A winding root, stemming and sprouting

In multiple directions, towards the sunlight.

08/09/18

Interrogation

The use of derogatory terms,

Expressed by those of the same nature,

Reinforcing it as culturally acceptable,

Neglecting many years of referendum.

It's a mystery why equality cannot be the motive.

A Survivor of a Metaphorical War

Blind-sighted to a clear definition of the world,

Surviving through natural disasters,

In addition to sustaining the ability to fly, without wings.

A being soaring through the sunset sky;

Hoping for freedom from a post-war catastrophe.

Review

Learning to understand a character is quite demanding at times. It often expresses itself as a snowball effect. The outside world only sees the tip of the iceberg, winding down like a Jack-in-the-box. However, the Jack-in-the-box never stays still; it continuously jumps back up.

Why is this character so hard to understand?

Do other people perceive them like this?

They look happy – or is it just a brave face?

Do you recognise your value?

You walk upon a battlefield in a confined space, with nowhere to turn. The people guiding you towards a safe haven are phenomenal and truly a blessing. This does not come easily in a competitive environment.

Repetition of Emotions

Fight or Flight

Dripping – each water droplet echoing from the tap.

Tears – rolling down your exhausted face.

Surreal – and tranquillity is the norm.

Fatigue – legs collapsing beneath you.

Shock – an electric shock with a thriving impulse.

Subconscious – a survival response is activated.

The options of sleeping beauty or a racing wreck, seeing

RED.

Tears of Failure

Sprinting over a hurdle, each stride requires a degree of strength, will-power, and belief. The goal is making it to the other side, without falling. Nevertheless, a fall shocks us with the resilience and faith we need to get back up and continue running, towards the finishing line.

Solitude

Thoughts keep saying, 'Be the bigger person'.

But to suppress more emotions would let the cycle begin again.

Is there a point where this doesn't become hard?

You can heal your past, take relief of the ego

And obtain your confidence.

Doubtfulness

Tell yourself how well you are doing. The repetition of constant improvement will reduce these words to mumbles. Step into the unknown: this is the breakthrough that birthed this person – a person who has been longing to appear. Working towards being caught up with oneself leads to less of a need, for constant reassurance of worth and second-guessing. In the moment, a closed mind is the motive, sustaining breath to allow us to swim underwater. Although, in hindsight, the struggle was an illusion: within it nestled the treasure, waiting to break free.

Liberation

Don't put yourself in circumstances that pull you into a dark hole, leaving you drained and exhausted, like an anchor falls and plunges to the depths of the sea.

Let go! Be free!

Invest your precious time in sincerity. Experiencing win-win situations is truly authentic.

Being Sad

Allow yourself to be sad.

Process what you feel.

Understand the cause.

Express your emotions.

Transform and accept

All these regulations

To become liberal.

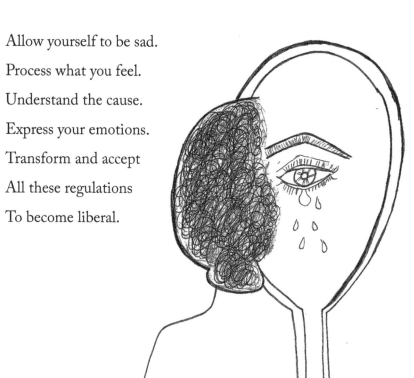

Deserving

Some analysis of your inner self is deserving; other thoughts are like a persistent cold. You need to adopt mechanisms to soothe the symptoms. It is okay to let thoughts and ideas resonate with you for a time, but believe me, do not squander your time by pondering indefinitely. A daily routine can help defeat this bug in your system: in your mind, body, and soul. You deserve to be healthy.

Vocal
Communication x
Triangulation

Lonely Bones

Flexing the arch of my feet,

In the position of plié; there sounds a snap –

The tibia connected to the knee bone.

Oh, how wonderful: another crackle.

A rusty waistline rotating, with the sound of a pop.

Not to hear a snap, crackle, nor pop

For a duration, would be magnificent.

These bones are aching,

Attached by joints, but oh! So

Lonely.

Alone Time

Daily struggles:

A daily fix? Jump-starting the day, filling it with productivity and positivity. Some days were easier than others, but was there a dependency for a visual haze? But routine was far from a habitué, and its illusion merely a placebo. I longed to become my best self, but remained disrupted by a suppressant to obtain my best analytical persona.

Strive to see true colours, like a rainbow appearing after rainfall, or the beaming sunrise. Continue watering your garden! After being concealed by four white walls and living on autopilot, accustomed to benefiting the workforce and unable to value oneself, those shoots and blooms will bring you back to yourself. Learn your personality: discovering traits, habits, triggers, and safe places is crucial.

Stereotypes

Like a monster destroying your entire universe, stereotypes overwhelm
us. Fearful of becoming a prey in an overpopulated city, constantly
analysing whether you have a sane mentality. Or, was a 'self-fulfilling
prophecy' being embraced?
Labels: boring, hypochondriac, over-thinker...
Opportunities enable liberation and freedom.
Your outlook on life can flutter frequently, lighting on different views
with papery wings,
Forcing your vision to transition from a blur to a 20:20 view,
Gradually building clarity,

And an understanding of purpose and strength within yourself.

Judging by perception

The mind feeling like a typewriter, processing information.

Each word relating to environmental stimulus.

The persistent grasp of overt attention.

It's intriguing how a lonely sunflower can be the talk of the town.

Perceptions can easily be misunderstood.

Petals are the only attraction to a swarm of bees.

The aesthetic of the growth period is not for everyone,

However, the central spirals provide

Raw, genuine, soulful nutrients, 365 days a year.

12.08.18

Understanding and intuition

You cannot expect applauses if you do not applaud yourself.

Always have a degree of humbleness.

The company of positive energy is a blessing,

Providing unmistakable courage.

Sustaining a timid persona,

Intertwined with a unique, glistening light.

Confidants

A decade of altercations, miscommunication and silence.

Always one; at each other's beck and call.

Learning to communicate sufficiently

And triangulate communication, via different domains.

As a collective, they are superior

And full of wisdom; lifting each other.

In this way,

Elevation to a higher purpose is routine

And nobody is left astray.

Dedicated to the beloved:

Flossy Possy

Wasps

Personal encounters

What are your hobbies?

Name three of your best qualities.

How would you describe yourself?

Each question elicits a memory, reconciled to self-evaluation. The cliché English language technique, 'point, evidence, explain', can be a useful inquisitive tool here. Pioneer your life decisions and responses, as slow and steady wins the race.

Worst days

Remember those who answered your calls

As well as messages.

Remember those who wiped your tearful cries.

Remember those who patiently waited for you to heal.

Remember on your happy days, a simple thank you

Will reside in the heart of those, who were there

On your worst days.

Pep Talk

If you continue to numb the pain

It becomes a hardship that is not necessary.

Stop

Silencing

Situations.

Sometimes it takes you disconnecting from reality,

Building your strength and expressing

Your emotions, to stop dwelling

In pity and burden.

Parley

ˈpɑːli/

noun

Shake off all the disputes from your shoulders.

Effective communication needs to sail through

Discussions.

An aggressive current cannot make your boat sink,

As long as the direction is mutual.

Relations, Associates and Friendships

A heart of pure gold. Does this exist? Not all intentions are pure. Many are corrupted by external factors and your humility can be taken advantage of. A hostile environment is unfit for you, especially when everyone speaks at once and expects you to translate. Over time, you will learn that some relationships come to a standstill and no longer progress. Acknowledgement of this is commendable. From this, other aspects of your life will begin to blossom like a miracle before your eyes. Nobody said life was easy, and lessons are visible, every day, in the problems that you face. You must decide to recognise these teachings and receive them, or the lesson will keep knocking at your door: reoccurring. The choice to better yourself is solely your responsibility. Don't become bitter to spite your tongue and dance with the enemy.

Almond
Blossoms *25:34 (33)*

History Repeating

Reflection: what is the definition of déjà vu?

Sometimes this may occur –

You experience encounters

And begin to recognise patterns.

Recollection may be admired when

Something, or an angelic being, breaks the cycle,

Creating a minor or intensive revolution.

Coasting

It all seems so easy; the turbulence of a lifestyle:

Missed transport and hours of procrastination.

Taking in surroundings. So much energy in one vehicle.

Linking the past to the present,

Trying to apprehend the future.

Before, signs approaching were London King's Cross

And now, signs approaching are Dover.

Coasting through,

Coasting past,

And coasting for eternity.

The calendar date reads:

The twenty-fourth of the eighth.

Once again.

Clouds

The heart begins to grow heavy; it can no longer bear excess pressure. The relief of anguish is released, and all negativity is lifted, after a crescendo of stress. Things take different forms, responding to various stimuli. The frequency of this phenomenon fluctuates, dependent on the seasons and the atmosphere.

Ocean Waves

Therapeutic, as the motion of the sea is captured visually.

The changeable speed of the wind creates slow movement among the waves

Passing over your body,

Abolishing what no longer serves you.

The horizon between the ocean and the clouds is in the distance.

A weightless feather floats within the atmosphere, making you feel light

and delicate,

Slowly bringing you back to reality.

22:22

Two white butterflies fluoresce, gliding past the rear-view.

Religious symbology comes to mind:

'two white butterflies,

two white doves,

Appearing as a soulful connection

And protection for life'

Lavender Essence
for Amethyst
31.08.2018

Stepping into the Abyss

Social Media:

Everyone has their ideology.

It can be beneficial and a curse at the same time.

Travelling to different continents and embracing cultural immersion is a luxury and an invaluable experience. First-hand history is fundamental for your mental health and well-being. It broadens the spectrum of your knowledge, regarding the world we live in.

Examples:

Cultural norms and values

Foundations of cities

Indigenous tribes

Communication

Festivals

Foods

Research

Limitless findings.

Always something to learn.

Navigate your meaning.

Seek advice.

Find like-minded resources.

There's always hope,

providing you try.

10%

The historical myth that humans only use 10% of their brain capacity is quite interesting.

Imagination, explanation and discussions.

Limited and inaccessible literature.

Monitoring and controlling of what's planted, in your peripheral view,

Comprehension requires curiosity and patience,

Coinciding with increased brain power.

There is a necessity of progression and regression for germination,

Whilst being an inhabitant on defiled lands.

Check-In

Constantly supporting others by filling their life up with abundance.

But,

Do you love yourself wholeheartedly?

If not, is it an acquisition of unhappiness?

Do you check in with yourself?

Accountability

V.O.I.D

Coming to crossroads.

Living in your truth.

Some situations become

null or cancelled.

Don't confuse this junction

Of self-love

With the avenue to

Egocentricity.

Detours

In the journey of your life

Mistakes can cause detours.

A source for a lesson,

Sprinkled with compliance.

Actions

The same way you keep an open heart and mind,

Continue being authentic with yourself.

You are the real MVP! A boss concurring the world!

Even during the blizzard and storm of your past problems, you held your head high. You are stronger and more grounded than ever before. Believe this, even when you have a glimpse of thinking otherwise.

25/10/18

Marche

One foot in front of the other.

Balance your core for structure.

Practice for development.

If you don't rise up

You'll continue crawling through life.

Utilise your surroundings for support.

Stretch those ligaments and reach for your

GOALS!

Decorum

Dining

Build and create a seat at your table. Embrace the feelings of growth, happiness, and faith. You will continue to be lost trying to understand a whole menu. Choose what is familiar or something brand new? It's the norm to stick with familiarity. Nevertheless, red wine can wet your palette, prompting you to discover, evaluate, and adapt to something new.

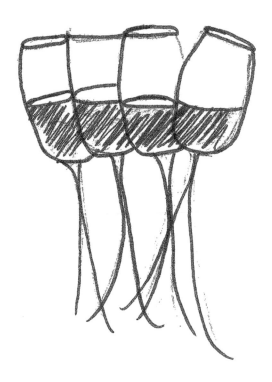

Boulogne-Billancourt

Accustomed to entrepreneurship.

Somehow, it's a lifestyle.

Re-evolving into a human being,

Juxtaposed with simply being human.

Take heed:

Experiment with

BEING.

Concrete Jungle

Concrete Jungles

Filled with history.

Here but coasting from reality.

Vivid dreams of a fantasy.

For pure bliss, in addition to

SIMPLICITY.

Happiness

It is with you.

Within all your power.

A coffee filter resists all residue, under pressure,

Requiring change and maintenance.

Filter your thoughts; begin to take charge

Of your joy and righteousness.

Crossword

Available clues,

Modify your introspection.

Paradigms of routes –

A horizontal and diagonal

Gateway,

Rejoicing all quarters.

Sunflower

Tower of Reinforcement

Be: Open

Be: Worthy

Be: Faithful

Be: Present

Be: Humble

Be: Grateful

Be: Creative

Be: Amazing

Be: Resilient

Be: Confident

Be: Optimistic

Be: Self Aware

Be: Thoughtful

Be: Determined

Be: Empowered

Be: Independent

Comfort

Two hearts beating as one.

A connection with a strong core.

Manipulation is not necessary.

A magnetic field will not resist

The temptation of attraction.

Metro Writing

Multitude

A container of collections.

We select what we admire first.

Working our way to the mediocre.

Leaving the last to wither

Collectively.

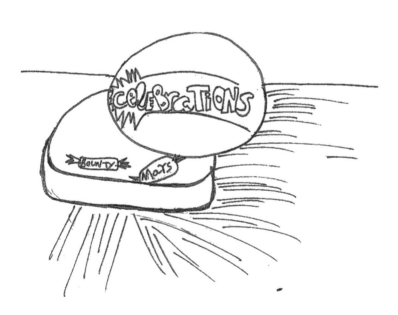

Troubled Waters

Maliciousness:

Everyone can take on this characteristic,

Raising sticks and stones,

But instead, it's an iron furnace to the heart.

Heartbreak is real and violent.

Expectations

Daily care: watering a sunflower.

Drench your aura

In alignment spiritually,

You grow boundaries to eliminate

Stress factors.

Mental Analysis

Revolution

Would you recognise a light bulb moment?

A blockage wiped away –

Have you ever felt this?

Networks come flooding in:

A route for your aspirations.

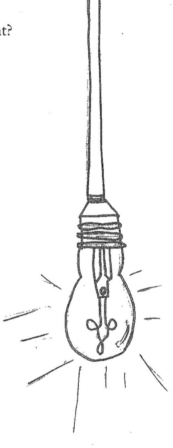

Façade

Incense

Imagery of what it used to be:

A scent instantly reminds you of their aura.

Memories of a fantasy, all extremely limited.

The fire reached the base swiftly,

A fragment of you enclosed in their destiny.

You can never forget the junior aroma.

Audio

Transporting you to another dimension.

Allow lyrical imagery to expand your mind and release your stress. Find peace.

A simple workout for your brain. Embrace key tools; determine your current mood and frequency to endure an emotional connection,

Often evoking nostalgia, essential when in a time of crisis.

Love

At times, love is a consideration of the past.

History and actions are taken without affection

Or understanding of the outcome:

A point where self-love and value are not cherished.

Yearning – for forgiveness.

We've all been there and unable to think, function, or breathe.

Head over heels

One superior; the other inferior.

Never on the same podium.

Never what you require.

Never what you appreciate.

Drowning in a tank of pity.

4-8 minutes.

A closed heart chakra. Your reflection staring back at you, directly into your cornea. It commenced with:

2 mins: speaking of gratefulness

1 min: understanding of self-love

2 mins: acknowledging and accepting flaws

1 min: apologising for negativity

2 mins: recognising and understanding your emotions and well-being

Remember, we are all human and make mistakes.

It's how you learn from these and keep sailing forward that is important.

No burden is entitled to your whole being.

Do not allow a menace to take away your freedom or happiness.

Speak positivity to yourself.

Opportunities will manifest around you.

There is no barrier to your accomplishments unless you allow it. You are your longest commitment in this lifetime, so keep sailing to paradise!

Biblical

Amnesia

For BCE (**Before Common Era**)

For BC (**Before Christ**)

For AD (**Anno Domini**)

A way of living.

Life beyond us.

Programmed to govern us.

Uninstall your bad habits

And let each day bloom with

GREATNESS.

Egalitarianism

It is not achievable in many domains.

To be the most content,

To be happy with simplicity.

Historically, Jesus turned WATER

into WINE.

Imagine sustaining this

Superhuman ability.

Black Attire

My attire is my expression.

I feel down, so I wear deep tones of blue and black.

Oh, are these tones too dark against my chocolate,

Mahogany skin?

Freedom of choice and earth colours in Printemps,

This woman's work.

My drive, desire and destiny.

Don't try to control my fragility,

Just for the pleasing of one angry bird.

Everything is perspective.

Unhappiness is overthinking.

Antiquity of failure is unknown.

Manipulation caused ramification, to serpents;

Universal customs create seasonal signs and calendars.

Hierarchy; the forefront routine and calendars, for their interests.

Salvation was there and prevalence, of serenity and truth.

Hidden gems to parables.

Source the clues and connections to lines, dots, and phrases.

Exclusion for inclusion.

Organise and concur – lowest requirements.

Defined 'soldier'.

Exposed – are those, lowest economically.

Prioritising – health and work.

Bravery through spiritual and developmental

Awakening – merciful souls.

Top to bottom.

Now read. Right to left.

Malarkey Happens, Keep the Faith

A sunflower has its peak season,

Just like you. Your peak season is near.

Soon you will blossom.

Don't block your light.

Dig deep and triumph.

Foreign Language

Do not follow the crowd.

The crowd is lost.

Mute, but varied understanding,

Find a means of communication.

Nothing is gibberish.

Rome was not built in a day,

So discard the weight of thinking

This is achievable overnight.

Persevere.

Remain humble, as

Love conquers all.

Famille

Your entourage.

Creating comprehension of your life's direction.

Viewing your background and the slavery of reality.

Your social network.

The initial group of individuals before expansion into society.

Articulation prevents intolerance and confusion.

In contrast,

Let them with ears acknowledge the spoken word,

And others only acquire selective knowledge.

Guardian angel:

The root of the branches. An olive tree with foundation.

Healing from the inside out; the Most High changing your experience.

Interior persona –

Do not let it be tarnished.

Emotional warfare.

Let me reintroduce myself.

Inspired by Lauryn Hill MTV Unplugged No. 2.0.

Acknowledgements

Creating these words has been a rocky journey. Thank you to those who have taken the time and energy to read these pages filled with trauma, assurance, and faith. Each page was made to analyse a pathway to personal elevation.

I am ecstatic that I have created a book. To those whom I have met throughout the last few years, I would like to reiterate my biggest thanks for their teaching, encouragement, and guidance. If I were to acknowledge everyone, I would be here for a while, but special thanks must go to my family, friends, mentors, and work colleagues. You are all a blessing from above – in other words, to quote one of my poems, **THE REAL MVPs.**

There should be no limit to your objectives or your achievements. Dig deep and find your purpose through a combination of struggles, aspirations, and goals. For a long period, I was oblivious to what my hobbies were, when they were right in front of me. Silence can be your best friend, turning every problem into a souvenir.

In the near future, I hope to create an in-depth podcast or video in which I discuss my perspective of these quotes for my readers. Until then, allow these words to be open to interpretation, solve the riddle of your own heart, and continue to be resilient!

About the Author

Lakieshia Stapleton Jelenke is a 23-year-old up-and-coming writer specialising in the welfare of children. Through exploring the issues surrounding one's mental health, living through traumatic events, and dealing with 21st century problems, her writing is a hopeful roadmap to remaining resilient and faithful despite what's happening in the world. This collection reflects the ending of an era in her life where she faced excessive doubt and abundant stress, and ultimately rose above it all.

In December 2018, the author published one of her first quotes on Instagram, taking the first step on her writing journey. *Arising Sunflower. Lost in Translation* is her first book. Her great creative influences include writers such as Maya Angelou, James Baldwin, Michelle Obama, Susan Jeffers, Raupi Kaur, Pierre Jeanty, and Reyna Biddy. Musically, her main inspirations are Lauryn Hill, Kehlani, India Aire, Jhene Aiko, Mahalia, and Emeli Sandé.

Connect with the author on Instagram and Facebook:
@remyantoinettethepoet

Lightning Source UK Ltd.
Milton Keynes UK
UKHW020000180720
366651UK00008B/81

9 781649 218315